The Truth About Who We Are

The Truth About Who We Are

Letter to My Grandchildren

DOUGLAS J. BROUWER

RESOURCE *Publications* • Eugene, Oregon

THE TRUTH ABOUT WHO WE ARE
Letter to My Grandchildren

Resource Publications
An Imprint of Wipf and Stock Publishers
199 W. 8th Ave., Suite 3
Eugene, OR 97401

www.wipfandstock.com

PAPERBACK ISBN: 978-1-5326-6096-2
HARDCOVER ISBN: 978-1-5326-6097-9
EBOOK ISBN: 978-1-5326-6098-6

Manufactured in the U.S.A.   OCTOBER 8, 2018

For Sarah and Elizabeth

Our Calvinist fathers wore neckties with their bib-overalls and straw hats, a touch of glory with their humility. They rode their horse-drawn corn planters like chariots, planting the corn in straight rows...

From "Calvinist Farming," *Purpaleanie and other Permutations*, by Sietze Buning

Contents

Acknowledgments

EVERY CHAPTER IN THIS book is, in a sense, an acknowledgment. When I examined the lives of my parents, grandparents, great-grandparents, and others, they turned out to be courageous in a way that startled me and made me proud to be descended from them. I am happy to acknowledge them with the publication of this book and thank them for the sacrifices they made and the example they have set for me.

When I started the research into my family history, I expected the work to be lonely, and, to be clear, much of the work involved long hours of tedious reading in historical records–baptism and marriage records, death certificates and grave locations, even ship manifests. But one of the most unexpected and satisfying aspects of the work turned out to be my experiences of collaboration along the way.

I am grateful to my mother, Ruth Wieland Brouwer, who accompanied me to cemeteries around Grand Rapids, Michigan, and patiently answered all of my questions about family history. I certainly hope my own children do not decide to ambush me at some point in my nineties with detailed questions about my past.

At ninety-one years old my mother was my closest link to relatives who are no longer with us and to various events I asked about. I should mention that at one point her memory of an important incident was sharply different from my own. When my grandfather–"Grandpa Pete"–stormed out of church during a sermon with an audible word of rebuke for the preacher, I remember being a child attending an evening worship service in Holland, Michigan. My mother, however, remembers that the incident occurred at a church in the Hague, when I was seventeen years old, visiting my grandparents in the Netherlands. She is as firmly committed to her memory as I am to mine. But this is my book, and in the end I recorded what happened as I remember it.

Another collaborator was my friend James M. Leunk. Jim and I were college roommates, and we served together on the editorial staff of *Chimes*, which at one time was an extraordinary college newspaper. I remember Jim as an exacting editor who did not suffer fools (or bad writers) gladly. His thorough reading of my book brought back memories of our newspaper days and reminded me why he was the only member of that newspaper staff to pursue a career in editorial work, mostly but not exclusively with Gannett newspapers. He and I share the Dutch immigrant experiences I describe in this book, and it's important to say that Jim's feelings about that history are markedly different from my own. I am glad for our conversation one day–at the Windmill Restaurant in downtown Holland–which served to sharpen my thinking and renew our friendship, which has endured for nearly 50 years.

My brother–in–law, Marvin Hage, is a physician who practiced obstetrics for many years and later taught on the faculty at the Duke University School of Medicine. Because he lives nearby and because he shares an interest in family history, he read chapters and offered encouragement. He was often able to help me sort out inevitable questions about health problems and causes of death. Reading death certificates from a hundred years ago, for example, would have been impossible without his insights and patient explanations. Another brother–in–law, Wesley Richard DeYoung, is no stranger to family histories, having done similar work several years ago, and he too offered helpful advice. Knowing the grandchildren to whom this letter is addressed, Dick was a strong advocate for speaking to them plainly and honestly.

My daughters, Sarah and Elizabeth, to whom the book is dedicated, read chapters as I completed them and offered their helpful advice and encouragement. My younger daughter was unsparing in her criticism of my occasional math and science problems. I didn't always like her observations at the time, and told her so, but now am more grateful than I can say that she saved me from embarrassing myself. If errors remain, they are my responsibility and mine alone.

And of course thank you to my editor at Wipf & Stock, George Callihan, who was terrific—patient, accommodating, and thorough.

It is to the beautiful children Sarah and Elizabeth brought into the world, and into my life, that this book is addressed.

Introduction

To my beautiful, awesome, amazing, smart, and utterly adorable grandchildren,

I would use each of your names in addressing this letter to you, but I suspect that there may be one or two more of you who come along after I finish. At least that's what I'm hoping, and I don't want to leave out anyone.

You won't know until you have a grandchild of your own how thrilling it is to be a grandparent. That was true for me, and I suspect it's true for most grandparents. I hope someday you have the same experience.

Some of the thrill of being a grandparent, at least for me, has to do with my experience of being a grandchild. I learned through my grandparents what unconditional love feels like, and I can tell you there is nothing in all the world quite like it.

Because it felt so good to me, I was determined to share as much of it as I could with you.

Whenever I hold you, there is so much I would like to tell you, but I realize that you aren't able to listen just yet. You just want to be held, fed, changed, and treated like the most important person in the world. And to me you are. So, instead of boring you with my stories before you are ready to hear them—if you are ever ready to hear them—I decided to write this letter.

This letter doesn't contain everything I want to tell you, but it contains enough. You'll get the idea pretty quickly about me and what I think is important.

Please don't feel bad if this isn't of any interest to you. My grandfather (you'll meet Jay Brouwer and several more grandparents and great-grandparents if you keep reading) took me out to his garage one day and showed me his tool chest. Inside were some old and valuable tools which he had kept in perfect condition. He told me that he wanted me to have them, which I realize in hindsight was an expression of love. He wanted me to have something precious to him, maybe so that I would remember him every time I used one of his tools.

But instead of saying "thank you," which is what I should have said, I said something like, "I don't need tools."

Whatever my exact words, they weren't the best words I could have spoken at that moment. If he was hurt, he didn't show it. He just kept on loving me, which is easy for grandparents to do. If you don't want to read this letter, that's okay. I won't be hurt. I'll keep on loving you.

What's ahead, if you keep reading, is not the story of my life, though there are bits of that story in these pages. My life was interesting to me, but it may not be all that interesting to you. What's ahead is some work I did, after I retired, to remember who I am, to rediscover my identity, my *true* identity. I will explain later what I mean by that. For now I just want to say that what I found moved me to write this letter. After more than 60 years of doing other things, I remembered who I was and what an important identity I had been given. It's your identity too, as you'll see.

If you want to talk about any of this, you can call me anytime. I would love to hear from you.

Love, Pops

Jessie and Jay Brouwer in an undated photo with Henry Vander Veen (Jessie's father), who appears to be in a playful mood.

1

What Is Truth?

I DON'T KNOW WHAT your parents told you about me, but you can forget most of it.

I'll tell you right up front that what they told you about me is not worth knowing. I'm not saying they lied to you. I know them better than that. I've known them longer than you have, as a matter of fact. They're fine people. I sometimes cry when I see how well they've turned out, and from what I can see they love you as much as it's possible to love another human being.

No, the problem is not that they lied to you. The problem is the truth—the truth about me, about you, about all of us.

What is truth?

That's a question, as you know, that is at least as old as the Bible. Pontius Pilate, the Roman governor, asked Jesus that question one time. He just blurted it out, which is sometimes how important questions are asked. "What is truth?" Pilate said. And no one knows if he was being sarcastic when he said it, or exasperated, or if he kind of wanted to know the answer. I've always wanted it to be the latter. I've always wanted Pilate to be a seeker after truth, even if he most likely wasn't. I hope you are a seeker after truth.

Enough about Pilate, but you probably heard that I was a preacher back in the day, before you were old enough to go to church. That's why I sometimes mention a name like Pontius Pilate. I know a few more, like Mephibosheth and Nebuchadnezzar. Those odd-sounding names are biblical names, and they're important to know, as I'll get to later on.

You never saw me stand in a pulpit in front of a lot of people and carry on for twenty minutes—and sometimes longer than that. Maybe that's a good thing. I don't know. Maybe it's better that you know me as the white-haired guy who lives in Holland, Michigan, who comes to visit now and then, and who is as proud as can be to be your grandfather.

What I do know—and what I want you to know too—is that my being a preacher isn't the whole truth about me. I was a preacher, that's true. I worked in churches for most of my life, nearly forty years, which is a long time, and probably hard for you to imagine at your age. I did other things in churches besides preaching, like visiting sick people, for example, but preaching was a lot of what I did. I stood up there in the pulpit week after week and said what I knew to be true. Your parents probably said I was louder than I needed to be, and I probably was, but that's because I was passionate about the truth. I still am. And that's why I'm writing this to you.

So here's what I want you to know: I'm more than a preacher. Let's get that out of the way at the beginning, shall we? Don't get me wrong. I'm proud of what I did as a preacher—most of it—and I did it about as well as I could, but preacher doesn't define who I am. I was a runner too for more than thirty years—did you know that?—and it was fun, and I liked it, most of the time, and I sure gave a lot of time to it, hours and hours. But being a runner doesn't begin to define who I am. The truth about me is much bigger than that and much bigger than a lot of other things I did with my life. The truth is always bigger than anything you will ever do with your life.

That's one of the most important things I want you to know about truth. It's big. It commands our attention. We need to look in its direction now and then. We can ignore it for a while, I suppose, and we often do, but sooner or later it asks us to look again, to notice, to make sure we've got it.

Truth—and I believe this with all my heart—is all we really have.

Are you with me so far? This is important—the *truth* is important—and I want you to understand, so stay with me. I want you to know the truth about me. Not what your parents said about me, not what I did for work, and certainly not what I did to be fit, but who I am and how I got to be who I am. I want you to know where I came from, and who my parents and grandparents were. I'm going to mention some great-grandparents too, people I never met, like Anthony Cornelius Brouwer and Henry Vander Veen, so be prepared. I want you to know what it means to me to be the grandson of immigrants, people who came to this country on a boat with nothing much in their pockets and who worked hard all their lives at jobs I would never do, mostly so that I could have a better life than they did.

I want you to know some of the things they taught me because that's important too—things like the Heidelberg Catechism (we'll get to that), reading books, being curious about the world around us, not being afraid to ask questions (even when they are uncomfortable), not claiming to know too much (another way of saying be humble), standing up for what's right, risking failure, being willing to admit when you're wrong, always trying your best, never settling for second best, and always seeking after the truth.

In the pages that follow—this may be the longest letter you ever receive—I plan to tell you about your DNA (the part of it I am passing along to you), your ancestry, your history, and your name. This isn't the whole truth about you either, as we'll see, but for me it was a way to learn about the truth, to re-discover it, to get closer to it than I had ever been before. Everyone has a story, and this is mine, which means that it's your story too. We share this story, and that makes me happier than you'll ever know.

What you'll discover, as I did, when I did the research about who I am, is that we have a story, a history. We came from a place on the map. We came from the Netherlands, as a matter of fact, a tiny country in the northern part of Europe. They still have kings and queens, which always makes me smile when I think about it.

You can go there, walk around, and meet the people who still live there. Without much imagination you can see your family members there, people who look a lot like you and me—sturdy, big-boned, and (I'll just admit it) not especially attractive people. You can see the houses where your family members lived, the churches they attended, even the farms and shops where they worked. What was amazing and wonderful and at times overwhelming to me was that I found this to be a good place to be from. I looked around at everyone and everything and felt proud.

What I want you to know is that you can be proud of it too; you can own it, and no one can ever take it from you. My guess is that you will discover, as I did, the truth about yourself.

So let's get to that, shall we? What is truth? What is the truth about you?

The grave marker for Anthony Cornelius Brouwer, Fulton Street Cemetery, Grand Rapids, Michigan.

The death certificate for Corneelja Priscilla Brouwer. Note the name change to "Cornelia." "Corneelja" was the name she was given at baptism and is the name that appears on her grave marker. Dutch spellings were often changed on census forms, baptism records, and death certificates.

2

A Person Goes on a Journey

THE NOVELIST JOHN GARDNER famously said that "there are only two plots in all of literature: a person goes on a journey and a stranger comes to town."

I've decided that the story of my life is the first kind of plot.

After living the first twenty years of my life in Grand Rapids, Michigan, I moved away. I couldn't wait to go. Not because life in Grand Rapids was so bad—it wasn't—but because I felt a powerful urge to get out of there, to explore, to open myself to new people and new experiences.

I'm not the first young person ever to feel this urge, and I won't be the last. It's got to be tough on parents, too, as it would be for yours, but I knew what I had to do. I would have been miserable if I hadn't.

Princeton, New Jersey, is only 750 miles from Grand Rapids, a long day in the car, but it's not far as journeys go. I had already traveled much longer distances in my life—to Europe, for example, for three weeks, after I graduated from high school—but moving to Princeton was for me a big move, the biggest I could imagine at that point in my life. I said goodbye to everyone and everything I knew and set out for a school and a city I had never seen with my own eyes.

That may sound odd, because today people visit campuses and take a tour and then decide where to go to school based on solid information and first-hand impressions. But I set out not knowing what I was going to find. In addition to my letter of acceptance to Princeton Theological Seminary, I had an Oxford Annotated Revised Standard Version of the Bible my grandmother had given me and a large green spider plant my girlfriend had given me. That girlfriend would one day become my wife, the person you know as your grandmother.

As it turned out, Princeton was quite a nice place to live. But that move, I have to say, was the hardest thing I have ever done. I struggled. I had to make new friends. I had to figure out who I was in a place where no one knew me or my parents. And—because I went to a theological school that was very different in some ways from the tradition in which I was raised—I often had to figure out what I believed.

After class I would come back to my room in Alexander Hall, and I would be in a cold sweat, wondering how I was going to reconcile what I had just heard in class with what I remembered hearing when I was growing up. This didn't happen every day, but it happened on enough days. I may be wrong, but I have always thought being a law student must be easier than being a seminary student because learning the law isn't the same as examining your heart.

Anyway, for at least two years I found myself trying to figure out what I believed, often swimming against the current, thinking hard, struggling with what I heard, and of course seeing your grandmother during summer breaks, which did a lot to keep me going.

My journey, however, did not end with Princeton. There was more I needed to learn and see and discover—about the world and especially about myself. In the years after, I have traveled to Iowa (for a year), back to New Jersey (to finish the degree), to Pennsylvania, to New Jersey (again), then to Illinois, to Michigan (to Ann Arbor, not Grand Rapids, there's a difference), and finally to

Florida. That was a lot of moving and a lot of meeting new people and a lot of figuring out who I was.

I know some people who never leave the town where they grew up, and sometimes I'm jealous of them and wonder what it would have been like never to leave, to live my whole life in one place, to keep the same friends for a lifetime. And what I've decided is that there are losses in this life I chose for myself. I left behind some important things—not only friendships, but also roots, a feeling of permanence. For every new friend and exciting discovery, there was also a loss and a feeling of grief.

And yet I still wasn't finished. I had one more journey left in me. And so, just before turning sixty years old, an age when people should have things figured out for themselves, I set out again—this time for Europe. Before retiring and moving back to Michigan, which had been our plan, I moved to Zurich, Switzerland, where I lived and worked and, I must say, had the adventure of my life.

Your grandmother and I lived in Zurich for several years, I met people from all over the world, and I even learned to speak a new language while I was there, something I had always dreamed of doing.

I don't see any more journeys in this life, not like that, which is good news to your grandmother, but I now find myself thinking about what I did, all the places I lived, and what caused me to get up and go in the first place.

In my genealogical research, I made some interesting discoveries, some of which I will tell you about in this letter. One of the most interesting discoveries, I have to say, is how often the word "arrival" shows up in the records.

In addition to words like "birth," "baptism," "marriage," and "death," my research turned up this other word that was every bit as important for many of my ancestors. When I started exploring my family tree, I was able to find dates (and places) of birth, information about baptisms and marriages, dates of death, and sometimes even places of burial. What I didn't expect to find was this other date, when one of my ancestors arrived in the U.S. after a long and tiring transatlantic voyage.

Between 1815 and 1865, one of the largest migrations in history took place. Several million people set out for the U.S. from Europe. A third of them, during those years, came from a single country—Ireland —which suffered a terrible famine in the mid-nineteenth century. Another large group of immigrants—around five million—came from Germany.

Fewer came from the Netherlands, but the Dutch came as well, along with people from Italy, Poland, Austria, and Slovakia. Mostly they came for economic reasons, but a few of them, like my ancestors, came for religious reasons as well. They wanted to find work, but they also wanted to find a place where they could live out their rather strict interpretation of the Calvinist faith.

I have more to tell you about that faith in another chapter, so I will mention here only that what they did is astonishing to me. I give them credit. I think about the strength of my own faith, and I wonder if I would have been able to do what they did.

My own move to Europe was hard. I won't lie. For one thing, I missed your parents terribly. And I also missed everything that was familiar. But I had a few things that my ancestors didn't—like the internet. I also knew that one day I would move back to the U.S. At least weekly, because of the miracle of the internet, I could both see and talk to your parents. And you weren't aware, but I could see you too. Your grandmother and I hurt terribly not to be with you, but I loved seeing your faces. And I couldn't wait to move back so that I could be closer to you.

Part of the difficulty of making any journey is learning to speak a new language. Even if you never leave your own country, you find that the people you meet on your journeys speak a different language. Words you think you know sometimes have different meanings in different parts of the country. You have to listen carefully to understand what they are saying. I have tried to be a good listener wherever I lived.

If I had been a toddler, I would have become fluent in German within a few months of my arrival in Switzerland, but learning a language later in life, as studies have shown, is very nearly impossible. The brain just isn't wired that way. So, I will never sound like a native German speaker. My American accent is so pronounced that the people I met sometimes laughed when I spoke, which was not encouraging.

The point is, having journeyed to a different country and having attempted to learn a language, I am in awe of what my grandparents and great-grandparents did. Their journeys, I now realize, were far more difficult than any journey I ever took.

Whenever I moved to a new place, typically there were people waiting for me and anticipating my arrival. When I first arrived at the Zurich airport, church members were there to meet me and show me around. They tried to make my move as painless as possible. When my grandparents and great-grandparents arrived in the U.S, they were on their own. No one met them and translated for them and drove them to their new home.

Most of my relatives came to Ellis Island, and from the first moments in their new country they had to demonstrate that they were mentally competent and physically strong enough for manual labor.

New arrivals were interviewed in the Great Hall at Ellis Island, and most new arrivals assumed that the interview was the start of the screening process. But I have read that there was a long stairway to get to the Great Hall, and immigration officials watched carefully to find out who could make the climb—and of course who struggled. The vast majority of those who arrived in the U.S. were allowed to enter, but not everyone.

My grandmother, Minnie Glerum, was five years old when she arrived along with her family, on a ship called the Potsdam, at Ellis Island in New York Harbor, on September 3, 1907. She repeated the story well into her nineties about how her mother, my great-grandmother, Leentje Glerum, died a little more than a month after her arrival in the U.S., at the age of forty-two, as though I might have forgotten this heart-wrenching fact.

My grandmother lived to ninety-seven years old and never forgot that early loss or any of the other losses that occur when a person goes on a journey. Her journey changed her, just as mine has changed me. It has left scars and wrinkles and occasionally a deep sadness.

On the other hand, I would have been miserable if I hadn't set out for Princeton all those years ago.

The Great Hall at Ellis Island in New York Harbor.

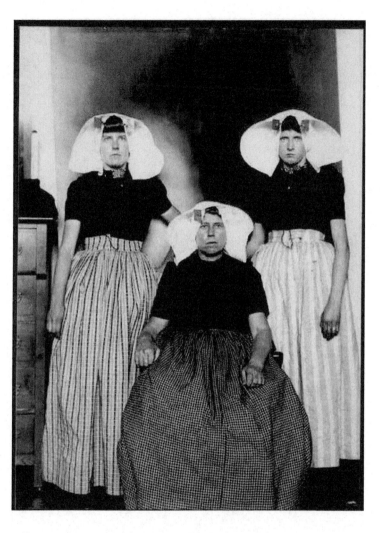

Three Dutch women. Portraits from Ellis Island, Augustus Sherman.

Dutch children. Portraits from Ellis Island, Augustus Sherman.

More Dutch children. Portraits from Ellis Island, Augustus Sherman.

SS Potsdam, Fred Pansing, oil on canvas (1844-1912).

3

There Is No Cure for Progonoplexia

I WISH I KNEW how to break this to you gently, but sometimes it's best to blurt out the truth: I have a common but nevertheless serious condition known as "progonoplexia." You might not have heard of it.

It's chronic and has no known cure. A combination of psychotherapy and low-dose aspirin seems to be the best treatment. At this point I am pain–free, and I want you to know that I intend to live a "normal" life for as long as I can.

So much for your grandfather's sense of humor.

"Progonoplexia" means, roughly speaking, ancestor obsession, which is what genealogical research surely is. Wikipedia actually deleted an article about this word not long ago because, in my opinion, the people who edit Wikipedia have no sense of humor.

You might say that *everyone* who engages in genealogical research suffers from at least a mild form of this condition. Some people obviously have more serious cases than others. Genealogical research, according to a recent survey, is the second most popular hobby in the U.S. today, just behind gardening.

Thankfully, my own obsession has been quite mild. (Never mind that "mild obsession" might be an oxymoron.)

People give lots of reasons for researching their family trees. Here are a few: to find out if they are related to someone famous, to discover the truth about family stories and legends, to trace medical conditions, to unearth a family inheritance (you are not, as far as I know, the heir to any beer fortune in the Netherlands or any other fortunes, but I will keep looking), to solve mysteries contained in family Bibles, to satisfy the tenets of your religion (if you're Mormon, mainly). There are many more.

My own reason for starting genealogical research was that I retired.

One of the reasons retired people like to do genealogical research is that they finally have the time, and occasionally it gives them an excuse to fly somewhere interesting for "further research," even though most research these days can be done easily and cheaply online. I have found all kinds of marriage and death certificates, church membership and baptism records, World War I draft registration cards, ship passenger and immigration lists, even grave locations, without ever leaving my desk.

My other reason for doing this, as I mentioned back in the first chapter, is that I wanted to find out who I am. Most people in their sixties, you might think, would know exactly who they are. And you're right, I should probably know who I am by now. But somewhere along the way, I lost track. My sense of self was buried somewhere. What it was, I think, is that I lived the life of a pastor so fully and for so long that I actually started to wonder if I had another self—deeper, less public, more authentic.

Looking into the past, a time before I was born, might seem like an odd place to look for my more authentic self, but that's what many people do. In family trees they claim to find helpful clues about who they are. My hope has been that the story of my family will help me remember who I am. In some ways it already has.

I'm not sure why I wasn't more interested earlier in my life. My mother (your great-grandmother Ruth Wieland Brouwer) has always had a collection of old photos hanging on a wall in her home, and I think she uses these photos the way I use my ancestor research. They tell her who she is each time she passes them.

To be honest, I used to be bored whenever she went through these old photos with me, one by one, and she probably knew that. I tried to appear interested, I really did, mostly because *she* was always so interested, but the truth is I couldn't wait to get out of there and do something else.

In those photos my ancestors all had serious, unsmiling faces, and their clothing was strange. They posed awkwardly with no apparent thought to composition. The whole point of each picture was never more, it seemed to me, than a photographic record that these people once existed. Frankly, I thought they could have been anyone's ancestors.

And then, in the last few months, all of that changed. I would come across a name—Anthony Cornelius Brouwer, for example, the great-grandfather who passed along the Brouwer name to me—and I would suddenly want to know about his life, thinking his life could help me understand my own.

A man born in the southern part of the Netherlands in 1858 suddenly had relevance for my life. I learned that in 1880 Anthony married a woman named Lena (or Leentje) Stoel, who was also born in the Netherlands. They immigrated to the United States in 1884, they had children, and finally they died.

Anthony lived to the ripe old age of sixty–five. Lena was fifty–three when she died.

Life expectancy then was not what it is today. Then, living into one's seventies meant living quite a long time. Women in my family tree often died much younger than men, mostly in childbirth, though there may have been other health factors as well, like flu and smallpox epidemics.

Comparing those ages at death with my own age today has reframed my thinking about getting older. Living another twenty years seems well within reach for me today, especially with the kind of health care available to me.

But I discovered something even more profound in my research about my great-grandparents, Anthony and Lena. They had six children which, I'll grant you, seems like a lot by today's standards. (It was more common then.) One of those children

—known only as "Baby Girl Brouwer"—was born July 3, 1903. The death certificate records that she was "stillborn." She was buried the next day—July 4, 1903—in the Fulton Street Cemetery in Grand Rapids, Michigan. I stood at her grave not long ago.

There is no marker for her, but records show that her body was placed in the same plot where her parents would one day be buried.

Another child, Cornelia Priscilla Brouwer, was born in 1894. She was the fourth of Anthony and Lena's six children. She died at age twenty, and her grave marker rests between those of her parents.

According to the death certificate, Cornelia most likely died of renal failure, after living much of her life with "cardiac asthma," which is not a form of asthma, but rather a heart condition with symptoms that mimic asthma, like a wheezing cough. It was not an easy way to die, not that there are a lot of easy ways to die, but for her parents it must have been painful and heartbreaking. Cornelia's mother, Lena, died less than two years later, and I wonder if there was a connection.

In my work as a pastor I have known parents who have lost children, which is a curious way to refer to something so difficult and painful. If you lose something like a house key, it's an inconvenience more than anything. But losing a child is something else entirely. One parent, after the death of a teenage daughter, said to me, "I wish I could cry a cry that was big enough, a cry that would finally get out all of the pain and grief." But there is no cry that is big enough for the loss of a child.

What's required is an inner strength and resilience that has no easy explanation.

One of the reasons some people do genealogical research, as I mentioned, is to find out if they're related to some heroic figure from the past. Even though there are no famous people in my family tree, there are a few people I deeply admire.

You've probably heard that we are all, in one way or another, related to Charlemagne, who lived way back in the eighth century and who fathered at least 18 children with various wives and concubines. I won't get into the reasons why everyone alive today who has some European genetic material is probably related to Charlemagne (hint: it has more to do with math than family trees), but Charlemagne will probably be the only truly famous person to appear in our tree.

That's okay, because I have found people in my tree—in your tree—who are worth remembering for a different reason.

Anthony and Lena had the courage to board a ship and come to a new country, with only the hope of a better life and with no hope of ever seeing the old country again. They experienced unspeakable pain and hardship along the way, as well as occasional joy and gladness. And (this is why I want you to know about them) they found a way to keep going, to persevere, with the support of their family and the strength of their faith.

I am Anthony and Lena's great-grandson and proud of it.

Lena and Anthony Brouwer in an undated photo.

4

Those Embarrassing Names

MANY OF THE PEOPLE I knew when I was growing up had rather odd–sounding names. Not distinguished–sounding at all, as I wanted them to be. The names were slightly embarrassing to me, as though in a previous life I had grown up with much better people, in a much higher social class.

There wasn't a Henry David Thoreau in my family tree. Or a Harriet Beecher Stowe, for that matter. Those names and a lot of others like them always sounded remarkable to me, as if you would want to know them and read their books and be like them.

Many of the odd-sounding names I heard belonged to my great aunts. There were Alice and Lena and Effie and even Trina. My grandmother was Minnie.

Minnie! Who names someone Minnie, unless it's the name of a cartoon mouse?

These were wonderful people. Don't get me wrong. They were always loving toward me, and they often demonstrated their love by making wonderful meals, usually at family picnics. I was a well–fed little boy.

One of my great aunts—I am pretty sure it was Aunt Effie, who lived to be a hundred and two—even slipped me a five dollar bill at my wedding reception and told me to have a nice breakfast "in the morning"—back when five dollars would buy a nice breakfast for two people. I will never forget that.

But it wasn't only the women in my family. Even some of the men had odd-sounding names. One of my favorites is Wiebe (who married a woman named Froukje a few generations back).

My grandfather, to give you another example, was simply Jay. Jay Brouwer. No middle name. He was Jay and never anything other than that. I loved him, and he loved me. He was about as proud of me as a grandfather could be, although my being the only grandson helped a little, I'm sure. But that name! What famous author—or president, or Nobel Prize winner—has ever had a name like that?

David Foster Wallace—now there's a name! And how about Louisa May Alcott?

But Jay Brouwer?

My grandfather never felt the need to add a middle initial as some of the people in my family tree apparently did. His mother, Lena S. Stoel, was married to Anthony Cornelius Brouwer, but her middle initial, as far as I could determine, didn't stand for anything. She was like Ulysses S. Grant, Harry S. Truman, and even J.K. Rowling. Not a middle name among them.

I felt a little short changed, to be honest, that I was not descended from a better class of people, with proper-sounding names.

For a lot of years I wondered about those names, and felt embarrassed about them, until I started reading widely and doing some careful research about my ancestors and how they came to this country.

What I found was not at all what I expected.

It turns out that those names I didn't like were often not the names their parents had chosen for them. When they were born, they had one name, and—some time later—it became something different. The change, as I saw it, was hardly ever an improvement. At one time Alice, for example, had been Altje. Effie had been Aafke. Trina had been Trientje. And so on.

My grandmother Minnie was given the name Jacomina at birth. Jacomina may not sound all that distinguished, I'll grant you, but at least it was an interesting name. I had never known anyone named Jacomina before. What happened? How in the world did Jacomina become Minnie?

Somehow I came to believe that the name–changing occurred during immigration. Poor, unsuspecting immigrants arrived on ships, and then, as I imagined it, uncaring officials at Ellis Island (where most but not all of them arrived) changed the names of the new arrivals to make them sound more American, less ethnic, but also less interesting.

My grandmother never said as much, but I detected something in her stories about coming to the U.S. that seemed to confirm this version of events. She used to tell me, for example, about being taunted on the playground by classmates who made fun of her Dutch language and her Dutch clothes and everything about her that seemed weird and foreign to them.

I just assumed that the name change was more of the same—the indignity of being an immigrant, a stranger in a strange land. I'd heard a lot of this sort of thing. But my reading and research turned up a much different story, one I think you should know. It touches me deeply, as so much of what I have discovered touches me.

Immigration officials did not change the names of people who were arriving. Those officials could be rude, and their uniforms were often frightening to immigrants. But most of the time they simply copied the names of those onboard from the ship's manifest. And rather than stumbling over the Altjes and Aafkes and Trientjes, it turns out that many of the Ellis Island immigration officials where themselves foreign-born. According to the U.S. Citizenship and Immigration Services, which was the name at the time, officials were fluent in an average of three languages. (I sometimes feel as though I am barely fluent in one.)

What I discovered was that immigration officials were assigned to inspect immigrants based on the languages they spoke, and if communication was difficult, interpreters (often from immigrant aid societies) were readily available. Most of these societies had offices in the Great Hall of the main Ellis Island building, a few steps from where those arrival interviews were taking place. So, if the name changes weren't a cruel introduction to life in the U.S., as I had always assumed, then what happened?

Well, it appears that most of the immigrants changed their own names ... *before* they left their countries of origin. Why? It's not hard to guess. Most likely they did it to get ready for assimilation into American life, to prepare themselves for what must have been the biggest, most difficult transition of their lives.

While they were saying goodbye to a country most of them would never see again, they were making the changes necessary to adapt and survive in a new country.

They changed the names their parents had chosen for them. Think about that.

When I lived in Europe, I discovered that my own name—Doug—sounded odd to the ears of German-speaking people. A Swiss friend pointed this out, as I was introducing myself one day. He said, "To these people your name sounds like the English word 'dog.'" And so, for a few years, I became Douglas to everyone I met. For me, of course, this change was hardly a difficult one, not like letting go of Jacomina to become Minnie.

As I type this, I feel a sudden rush of tears. Rather than being embarrassed by these people, I now find myself proud to be descended from them. I don't know if I would have had the courage to do what most of them did. I have more to tell you (in other chapters of this book) about their courage and strength, but for now let me just say that having a grandmother named Minnie makes me prouder than you will ever know.

I wish I had told her this when she was alive. I wish I could say thank you for all she did to prepare the way. To prepare the way for me—and for you.

Leentje and Jacob Glerum with my grandmother Jacomina (Minnie) in an undated photo.

Minnie and George Wieland on their wedding day, May 17, 1923.

5

My Name Is Brouwer

WHERE I GREW UP there was nothing at all unusual about the name Brouwer. Nearly everyone I knew—neighbors, classmates, teachers, even my pastor and dentist—had a distinctively Dutch last name, and so no one was ever puzzled by my name or had to ask me how to spell or pronounce it.

But as soon as I moved from Grand Rapids, Michigan, I quickly learned that Brouwer looked odd to some people and was hard-to-pronounce for others. The name has been misspelled in a dozen different ways, as you may already have experienced, and it nearly always raises a question, like "What kind of a name is that?"

What kind of a name is that? What kind of a *question* is that! Brouwer is a fine name, thank you very much, and I have always been proud of it, though for a long time I wasn't sure why.

The good news, I suppose, is that in history there have been no really disreputable people named Brouwer. That might have soured my feelings about the name. On the other hand, no one especially famous has been named Brouwer either, though a few people may come close.

There's a hockey player in the NHL whose name is Troy Brouwer. He seems to have played for every team in the league, which is an accomplishment. There's a Cuban-born composer and classical guitarist named Leo Brouwer. I discovered that his name is actually Juan Leovigildo Brouwer Mezquida, but professionally he uses Brouwer as his last name. Sigmund Brouwer is the name of a best-selling Canadian author of Christian books. He writes mostly for younger readers and has written more than thirty novels. Early in the twentieth century, there was an important Dutch mathematician named L.E.J. (Luitzen Egbertus Jan) Brouwer. I would like to read his books sometime, the ones not about math.

The only well-known woman I could find with the last name Brouwer was Bertha "Puck" Brouwer. She was an Olympic sprinter (for the Netherlands, naturally) and won a medal—a silver—in the 200-meter dash at the 1952 summer Olympics.

Probably the best known Brouwer who ever lived was a seventeenth-century Flemish painter named Adriaen Brouwer. I have known about him for most of my life because my parents had a coffee table book about him, and we always called him "Uncle Adriaen." Only a few dozen of his paintings have survived, but they hang in some of the best-known museums in the world, including the Metropolitan Museum of Art in New York and the Rijksmuseum in Amsterdam. The people he painted were, well, peasants—people who spent a lot of time (as he apparently did) in taverns—drinking, smoking, playing cards, brawling, and having their teeth pulled. He died when he was about thirty-three years old, and art historians attribute his early death to either alcohol abuse or the plague.

As far as I know, I am not related to any of the people I mentioned, not even "Uncle Adriaen."

When I was a child I tried to figure out what Dutch names meant. Most aren't hard to get. De Jong (some immigrants changed it to De Young) means "the young" or "junior." De Vries is easy too. It identifies a person from Friesland, a province in the northern part of the Netherlands. Van den Berg (also Van de Berg or Van der Berg) is kind of funny because it means "from (or of) the mountain," and as you know there are no mountains in the Netherlands; a third of the country is below sea level. Bakker is a common Dutch name, and—as with a lot of Dutch names—itrefers to an occupation—namely, "baker." Visser, likewise, means "fisher" or "fisherman." Mulder means "miller." A Meijer, Meier, or Meyer is an "overseer" or "steward." And Smit (often changed by immigrants to Smith) is—you guessed it—a "smith."

So, you won't be surprised to learn that a Brouwer is a "brewer"—of beer or ale. Back in the day, every Dutch village had a baker and a smith and most likely a brewer. People from all social classes in northern Europe drank beer, partly because growing grapes was difficult or impossible.

Beer is one of the oldest beverages humans have produced. It dates back to the fifth century BCE in Egypt and Mesopotamia. By the fourteenth and fifteenth centuries CE, European beer brewing had changed from being a family activity into something considered a skilled trade.

No stigma was attached to beer drinking either. Monasteries in Europe often sold beer and were some of its biggest producers, a bit of trivia that makes me smile.

How did occupations like baker and smith and brewer become last names? The answer, believe it or not, can be traced to a specific date and a famous person: The date is August 18, 1811, and the famous person was none other than Napoleon Bonaparte.

On that fateful day in August, with the French army occupying northern Europe, Napoleon signed a decree establishing a registry of births, marriages, and deaths. Families that did not already have a last name (or surname) were obliged to choose one. Say what you want about Napoleon, but he should be the patron saint of genealogists.

There's a legend, which I like, that some Dutch people resisted Napoleon by taking on goofy or nonsensical names, thinking they would simply drop them when the French army left. A few Dutch names I have heard seem to support this theory. What about Zonderkop (Without a Head) or Naaktgeboren (Born Naked) or Uittenbroek (Out of his Pants)? My personal favorite is Pekelharing (Pickled Herring), a Dutch delicacy.

Sadly, the legend is probably just a legend.

Centuries ago the Dutch also employed a patronymic system for names, which many Icelandic people still do (Icelanders also use a matronymic system). In a patronymic system the father's first name becomes the son's last name. If my family still used a patronymic system, my last name would be Jackson, because I am Jack's son. This explains why some Dutch people today have the names Jansen or Hendriksen or Klassen.

Rembrandt Harmenzoon van Rijn, a Dutch name you have probably heard, used the patronymic system. He was the son (or zoon) of Harmen, from the Rhine River, and interestingly he has no last name.

All of this is important to my story because, in my family tree, the name Brouwer first appears with a man named Rinze Davids Brouwer, my great, great, great, great-grandfather (four greats!), who lived from 1779 to 1839. Curiously, his father does not use Brouwer as a last name, and until I read the story about Napoleon, I had no idea how to account for the abrupt name change. Now, at last, there seems to be a reasonable explanation. The name Brouwer first appeared in my family tree on or about 1811, which is not all that long ago.

You probably already know that a name is not the most important thing about a person. "What's in a name?" Juliet once asked, in William Shakespeare's *Romeo and Juliet*. "That which we call a rose/By any other name would smell as sweet." And that's true. Who and what you are is far more important than what you are called.

Still, no offense to Juliet, names are important. Some people hate the one they were given and adopt something different. Others struggle to live up to the name they were given. A dear friend of mine who grew up in a Hindu village in India had to give up his family name when he became a Christian, something that reminds him every day about the extraordinary demands of his faith.

For me the name Brouwer is a reminder that I have a unique history, that the people who went before me worked hard and learned an important skill. I like to think that Brouwer is a solid name, and not at all flashy. It's earthy and unpretentious. In fact, I can make of it whatever I choose, good or bad.

If your parents gave you Brouwer as your middle name, then I hope you will think of it proudly, as I do. I hope you will remember that you came from good and solid and unpretentious people.

Adriaen Brouwer (1605-1638), The Bitter Potion.

6

You Are More Than Your DNA

YOUR PARENTS MAY HAVE told you that I'm not impulsive, that I am in fact quite deliberate, that I always like to dip my toe in the water before diving in. That is true. I tend to think things through before I speak or act.

Which is why I surprised myself and everyone who knows me when one day not long ago I gave in to an impulse and bought one of those DNA testing kits. I spit into a glass tube and then sealed it up and mailed it to a lab somewhere in California, so that I ... but that's the question. So that I could do what? What was I hoping to learn about myself?

DNA, as you know, is desoxyribonucleic acid.

Already you're thinking that you're not going to like this chapter—unless of course you turned out to have more of a scientific mind than your parents, in which case you're going to be curious to find out how much your grandfather really knows about this stuff.

DNA—this is as technical as I plan to get—is found in nearly every cell of your body, and it contains your unique genetic code. In other words, DNA explains why you are you.

Except that it doesn't.

DNA can explain a great deal, it's true—far more than I ever imagined. The information contained in your DNA is astonishing by any measure.

Francis Collins, the physician who led the project that first mapped the human genome, once called our genetic code "the language of God." He says that his study led him to faith in God. To examine who we are at this level is to hear, Collins explains, God's voice in our lives.

But if that's true, what exactly is God saying? I'm not sure.

The most basic thing DNA can tell you, of course, is whether you are male or female. And then of course there are eye color and hair color and a host of other characteristics that make you a truly unique person.

Even that detail at the beginning of the chapter about impulsiveness? Apparently a gene on the X chromosome that codes for the monoamine oxidase enzyme has certain versions associated with—you guessed it—sensation seeking and impulsive tendencies. I must have a deficit of that particular enzyme, which is remarkable when you think about it. My DNA seems to have predicted this particular trait.

On other hand, a great deal of who we are cannot be explained by our DNA. Race and ethnicity, for example, cannot be determined by a study of our DNA, a statement I had to read a few times to absorb fully. Our identity, it turns out, is shaped only in part by our genes. Genes can be turned on and off or ramped up and down by signals from the environment—and that's before we discover all the ways in which learning shapes personality traits and the brain.

For now, I simply want to let you know what I found out about myself by having my DNA tested. These results, after all, are part of your story as well.

As you know, I do not have blue eyes and blond hair. Many people who are born in the Netherlands—or trace their ancestry to that country—have those characteristics. So, I have always wondered, "How come I have hazel eyes and brown hair? Or rather, how come I once had brown hair? Could it be that some of my ancestors came from somewhere else—like Spain? Did one of my Dutch great, great great–grandmothers meet a handsome Spaniard and, uh, add a new wrinkle to my DNA code?"

The answer, unfortunately, is not nearly as interesting as my imagination wanted it to be. Overwhelmingly, my DNA matches up with people who come from the northern part of Europe— what is now called the Netherlands, Belgium, and Germany. There is even, as you can see below, a dash of "Scandinavia" in the mix. But no Spain, very little eastern Europe, and certainly no Africa or Asia.

If you look at a map of my DNA matches, you will see that all of my ancestors came from a surprisingly small strip of land, much smaller than the state of Michigan. Here's the breakdown from my DNA test:

ETHNICITY ESTIMATE

- Great Britain—80 percent
- Scandinavia—6 percent
- Europe West—6 percent
- Finland/Northwest Russia—4 percent
- Europe East—3 percent
- And the rest? The remaining 1 percent was attributed to "low-confidence regions."

You will notice right away, as I did, that 80 percent of my DNA matches occur in the region described by the testing service as Great Britain, and I had some fun initially telling everyone that I was actually British, had always loved tea, and might adopt a (faux) Cambridge accent.

The truth, which is not quite as much fun, is that Great Britain, as the DNA testing company defines it, includes that northern-most part of western Europe where we now find the Netherlands,

Belgium, and Germany. And no DNA matches were found on the northern (or U.K.) side of the English Channel.

So one mystery was solved. My parents told me I was Dutch, I always considered myself to be Dutch, and now my DNA confirms that I am Dutch—or at least that most of my ancestors came from the part of the European continent now known as the Netherlands.

In case you're interested, one of my sisters (your great aunt Linda) took the same test and had similar results.

You might say, "Well, of course she had similar results. She's your sister!"

But in your high school biology class you will one day learn that we get half of our DNA from our mothers and half from our fathers. (Actually we get slightly more DNA from our *mothers* for reasons I don't fully understand.) My sister, however, did not inherit the *same* half that I did from each parent. If she had, if she and I each received exactly the same 50 percent from each parent, we would be identical. But of course we're not. We're alike in some ways and very different in others. Each of us received a different combination of that genetic material.

Here's something else you might be interested to know. When I sent off my saliva sample to be tested, I elected not to receive any medical information. DNA can tell us if we're predisposed to develop breast cancer, for example, or dementia, or even heart disease and diabetes and unibrow.

I elected not to know. You might want to choose differently, if you ever get your DNA tested. You might want to know, for example, if you're more likely than the rest of the population to develop Alzheimer's disease. I figured I would find out soon enough and didn't have to know right now.

I'll tell you what else I elected not to know. DNA testing can help people find relatives they didn't know they had, what one DNA testing service calls "surprise relatives." I suppose this could be a good choice for adopted children, who want to initiate contact with their birth parents.

But DNA testing services also warn that finding out about these "surprise relatives" can be disturbing. Every day, as these testing kits become more affordable, I read another story of a surprised (and sometimes devastated) person who discovers, for example, that the person she thought of as her father is not her biological father. Long–hidden family secrets are being exposed.

So, if you do it, if you are thinking about having your DNA tested, you should consider your decision carefully (and suppress that MAO enzyme I mentioned).

In the end, I decided that the relatives I know about are surprising enough, which I mean in the nicest possible way. I've already mentioned a few of them and will mention a few more in the chapters that follow.

What I want you to know, more than anything, is that you are much more than your DNA. Your identity, the truth about you, is more than the DNA you inherited from me.

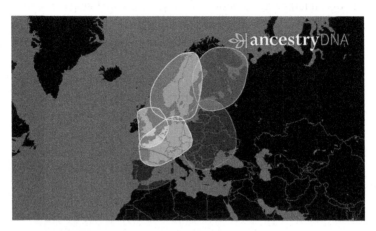

DNA Story for Douglas

- Great Britain   80%
- Scandinavia   6%
- Europe West   6%
- Finland/Northwest Russia   4%
- Europe East   3%
- Iberian Peninsula   <1%

7

Genealogies in the Bible

To be honest, I have never preached a sermon about genealogies in the Bible, not once in forty years of preaching sermons. How this happened isn't hard to explain.

I thought biblical genealogies were a waste of time. I always found them boring and repetitive, certainly too tedious to be read aloud in a church service. And frankly, I thought, who really cares that "to Enoch was born Irad, and Irad was the father of Mehujael, and Mehujael was the father of Methushael, and Methushael was the father of Lamech"?

That's in Genesis 4:18, if you want to look it up. I'm guessing that no one ever memorizes that verse or uses it for personal devotions. Now that you know something about your grandfather's sense of humor, you will understand that I would love some inspirational wall art (or pillow) with that Bible verse, an inexpensive Christmas gift!

Also, you'll notice that women never seem to play much of a role in a biblical genealogy. When women are mentioned, as they are in Matthew's genealogy of Jesus, they play a secondary role, so apparently inconsequential in fact that Bathsheba, the mother of Solomon, is not mentioned by name. Matthew 1:6 refers to her only as "Uriah's wife." That's a short resume.

If you know anything about your grandmother, then you know she would like to be more than "Doug's wife."

There is one interesting characteristic you should notice about the women mentioned in Matthew's genealogy —Tamar, Rahab, Ruth, and Bathsheba. They were foreigners. Matthew thought it was important to mention that in the genealogy of Jesus there were outsiders, people outside the clan, the tribe, the chosen people of God.

I want you to notice this, because one of the important truths of the Bible is that God, unlike most of us, loves the outsider, the one who does not fit in. We tend to keep our distance from people who are not like us, but God does not. God always seems to be going out of God's way to include people like that, even in the family tree.

So far, in my own genealogical research, I haven't found any outsiders. In my family tree, everyone seems to have married within the clan, the Dutch tribe, usually within the same village, which makes research much easier. My DNA analysis would have uncovered any outsiders in the tree, and so far at least there is no one who fits that description.

On the other hand—maybe you can take some pride in this— my entire family tree is made up of outsiders, people who didn't fit in, who were poor and desperate enough to get on a ship, say goodbye to family and friends, and sail to the other side of the ocean. No one famous turned up in my family tree, no authors or political leaders or business tycoons, certainly no royalty. I don't mean to be harsh when I put it this way, but we are people of no account.

The historian James D. Bratt, in his fine book about Dutch migration to the United States, describes those who came as "a mass exodus of the rural poor," hardly a glowing description.

When I look at my family tree I see people only God could love—not because they are bad people, but because they aren't known for anything. They lived, they married, they "begat" children (to use the language of biblical genealogies), and they died. There's nothing terribly exciting in that from a historical or genealogical point of view, but those are the people, the Bible seems to say, whom God loves and cares about.

This reminds me—as a lifelong preacher, this is how my mind works—of a verse from Isaiah (53:2) where the prophet describes someone—known only as "the servant"—as having "no beauty or majesty to attract us to him, nothing in his appearance that we should desire him." Christians have always taken this to be a reference to Jesus, and I believe it is, but it could also be a reference to any of us, to you or me. No beauty or majesty. Nothing about us that would make anyone desire us. And yet, important—desirable—to God.

If you are still with me, there's something more I want you to see in biblical genealogies—namely, that their historical value is questionable.

Until the nineteenth century CE no one thought to question the accuracy and reliability of the genealogies in the Bible. In fact, they were considered to be remarkable records of the generations of God's people.

And then, in the late nineteenth century, biblical scholars noticed something that no one had noticed before. Most ancient Near Eastern cultures also used genealogies in their sacred texts. These biblical scholars began to compare the genealogies in our Bible with their counterparts in other sacred texts, and of course they found some striking similarities and some striking differences.

One of their discoveries—and I'll use the words of Robert R. Wilson, a Yale University scholar who has written one of the classic books about biblical genealogies—is that "in general, the makers of genealogies are not historians." Their purpose "in general" was often something different from writing history.

I'm not the first person to notice that the genealogies of Jesus in Matthew 1 and Luke 3 are quite different, and in spite of heroic attempts to harmonize them, serious differences remain. But what if an historically accurate genealogy was not uppermost on Matthew's or Luke's mind? What if our concern—historicity, reliability—was not theirs?

Think of it this way: My own genealogical research is as good as I can make it, given the tools I have (and the tools at my disposal are vastly superior to anything available to Matthew or Luke), but no one should ever look to my genealogical research as reliable historical fact. Nor was that ever my intent.

For example, I have found two people named Anthony Cornelius Brouwer who have similar birth dates and two entirely different sets of descendants. One Anthony immigrated to the U.S., and one apparently did not. I did the best I could to make sense of what I found (and even corresponded with someone in the other family tree), but in the end I had to decide what to include concerning one of my great-grandfathers, the one from whom I get my last name.

The mystery of the two Anthonys will most likely have to remain a mystery, and my family tree is only as reliable as I could make it.

Similarly, Matthew's intent seems to be to make the case that Jesus is the legitimate heir to the throne of David, something that would have been important to his readers. To get there he has arranged Jesus' genealogy into three groups—from Abraham to David, from Solomon to the Exile, and from the Exile to Jesus, two groups of fourteen generations and a third group with only thirteen generations, culminating in the birth of the Messiah.

For comparison, Luke created eleven groups of seven names, which is also an elegant way to construct a family tree. Luke's intent was also theological. Just as the disciples needed a twelfth disciple to be complete, as Luke tells the story in the Book of Acts (1:12-26), so history needs a twelfth group to make the family tree complete. We are the twelfth group in Jesus' family tree.

And for all of that, I would like to nominate Matthew and Luke to the genealogist hall of fame.

To arrive at his remarkable and mostly-symmetrical family tree, however, Matthew omits four kings in the Davidic line, which would be a serious problem if his intent were simply an accurate historical record. But it's not. His intent, as I mentioned, was theological. He is doing his best to tell us that Jesus is the king like David we have been waiting for.

My intent, I have to say, was always far less grand than Matthew's (or Luke's). They were looking forward, using the family tree to make a claim about the future. I was looking backward to make a claim about the present. I was curious about where I came from. I wanted to know what I could learn about myself from the people who went before me.

If I have made some errors in constructing the family tree, which I undoubtedly have, I won't be surprised. I hope you will forgive me.

The greater truth, the truth that came as a pleasant surprise, is that you and are I descended from people that only God could love, and the good news is that God does love us. God has always loved people like us.

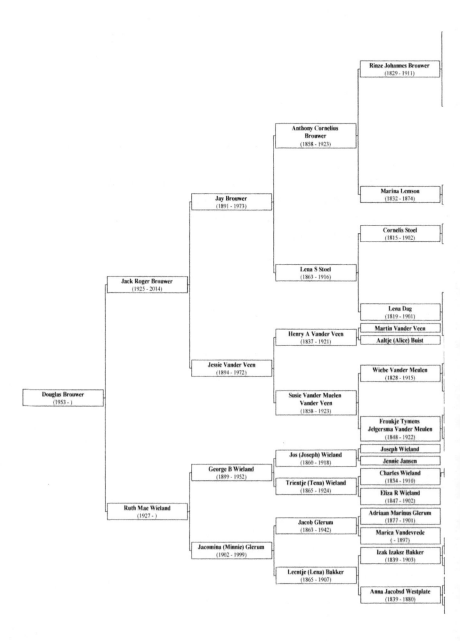

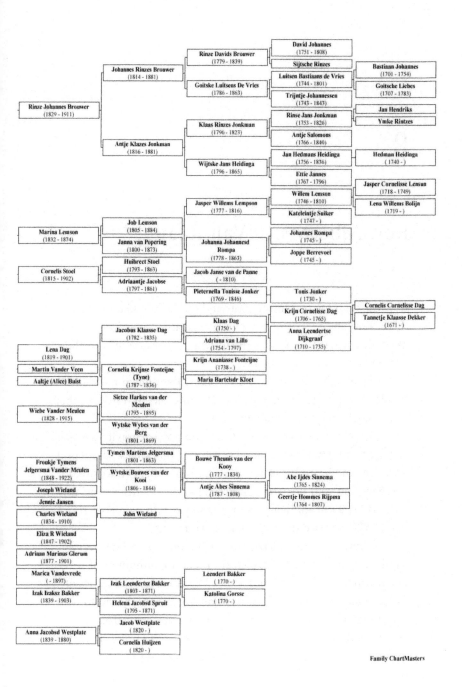

Family ChartMasters

51

8

Rev. Albertus C. Van Raalte

IF YOU ASKED DUTCH immigrants and their descendants whether there were any heroes of the Dutch migration, you would most likely get puzzled looks in return. Dutch immigrants and their descendants have few heroes.

The Dutch immigrants I have known are much more likely to offer harsh criticism than genuine thanks. Mostly, I believe, this can be attributed to our Calvinist faith.

If your starting point is the doctrine of total depravity—which teaches that human beings are incapable of choosing what is good and right and beautiful—then you are always inclined to look for evidence that your doctrine is correct. In other words, saying anything good about another person, possibly turning someone into a hero, feels like rejecting a key tenet of your faith.

I think that this doctrinal explanation goes a long way toward explaining why the Dutch immigrant community of western Michigan has few heroes—and why Albertus C. Van Raalte, in particular, receives so little recognition. When I began to read about him as part of my research about where I came from, I realized what an extraordinary role he had played in bringing Dutch immigrants to western Michigan and establishing a Dutch colony here.

His story is genuinely inspiring and heroic, but I never heard my parents or grandparents mention him. When I mentioned Van Raalte to my ninety-one year-old mother recently, she said, "Tell me again who he was." His role in Dutch migration to western Michigan was never taught in the Christian schools of my child-hood—or hers, apparently.

To be fair, there is a Van Raalte Institute dedicated to his-torical research at Hope College, in Holland, Michigan. There is also a 160-acre farm which bears his name, as does a street on the south side of the city. But this, it seems to me, is faint praise for a man who had such a courageous vision and seemingly boundless energy.

Van Raalte was born in the Netherlands, in the province called Overijssel, and he became a leader among the Dutch separatists, people who were concerned about the creeping liberalism of the Dutch church. And in 1847 Van Raalte led a group of separatists to the U.S. where they hoped to establish a Christian colony with freedom from all forms of government intervention in church life and worship.

Against long odds—food was scarce at the beginning, money soon ran out, disease and death were rampant—the Dutch com-munity in Holland quickly took root and thrived.

Dutch culture in the early twenty-first century sometimes has a kitschy feeling, especially during Holland's annual Tulip Time Festival, with its street scrubbing and klompen dancing, but the religious and economic vision of Van Raalte and his followers is very much in evidence. More than 170 churches, for example, can be found in a city with fewer than 34,000 residents. This figure does not include the churches found in surrounding Dutch com-munities known as Graafschap, Overisel, Drenthe, Zeeland, and Groningen. Today, Holland is rightly known as a "city of churches."

Pastors like to say that they "never took a course at seminary" in roof repair or heating system maintenance or fund raising, and for most of us that's true. The curriculum typically consists of bib-lical studies, theology, church history, and (sometimes) preaching. So getting involved in decisions about whether to replace or repair a roof, for example, always seems like a distraction from our spiritual calling.

If Van Raalte ever voiced similar complaints about his work and what constitutes a spiritual calling, those complaints were, as far as I know, never recorded. Van Raalte had a sense of vocation that was far exceeded anything I have ever contemplated.

After taking his group of immigrants by ship from Rotterdam to New York Harbor—and then as far west as Detroit, Michigan—he left most of them, including his wife and family, in Detroit for the winter months of 1846–1847.

Van Raalte's original goal had apparently been to settle in a major city, such as Chicago, Illinois, or Milwaukee, Wisconsin, where previous groups of Dutch immigrants had settled and where there would be plenty of homes and jobs. One historian has argued that Van Raalte actually had his sights set on Alto, Wisconsin, which is not near any major city, but where one of his former seminary students, Roelof Sleijster, had settled with a previous group of immigrants.

Whatever his original plans or intentions, Van Raalte began listening to several leading citizens in Michigan who were eager to have a group of hard-working, upstanding, and devout immigrants establish a colony in their state. So, with a few winter months to consider his options, Van Raalte set out for the west side of the state, going by train as far as Kalamazoo.

As a Presbyterian pastor I like to point out that it was the Rev. Ova P. Hoyt of the Presbyterian Church in Kalamazoo who strongly encouraged Van Raalte to consider settling on land in southern Ottawa County.

Van Raalte must have liked what he saw because he quickly arranged for the purchase of 7,000 acres near Black Lake, which is now called Lake Macatawa. There were no homes on this tract of land, no roads (except for a few trails), no villages with stores from which purchases could be made, no bridges over creeks and rivers, no business and industry, and no windmills for the grinding of grain or production of timber.

Most of the land, moreover, was heavily forested. The Native Americans who once lived in the area had cleared and cultivated only a few acres, so it could fairly be described as virgin wilderness filled with large trees. It was on this land that Van Raalte could imagine his vision becoming reality.

After a little more than a year in Holland, the *Detroit Free Press* reported, on July 10, 1848, that "there were about 200 houses of all descriptions, from the rude hut covered with bark, to the well finished and painted frame house, every lot occupied having a fine garden and yard, in front of the house a gate, and at every window on the street the neat white curtain."

Van Raalte and his followers may have been totally depraved, but they worked extremely hard. Their survival depended on their hard work, of course, but they did far more than survive. The extraordinary work ethic demonstrated in those first months continued well into the second and third generations of immigrant families.

This was the Dutch immigrant culture of western Michigan into which I was born a little more than a hundred years later.

It's important for you to know that I am the first member of my family to graduate from college. I graduated from Calvin College in 1975, close to 128 years after Van Raalte bought the land that was to be a Christian colony in Holland. The college I attended was not founded until 1876.

My father had the opportunity to attend college, but after high school he volunteered for military service and served in the Pacific during the last years of World War II. When he returned to western Michigan after the war, he had hoped to take advantage of the G.I. Bill, a law that allowed 7.8 million American veterans to receive educational benefits. My father never realized this dream.

I asked my father later in his life why he had not gone back to school after the war, and he told me he had been accepted by the Art Institute of Chicago, something I had not previously known. But his admission to the Art Institute had been delayed from September to January because of the large number of returning veterans.

At some point between September and January, my father met my mother and his plans changed. My father went to work instead of going to school, he and my mother were married, and very quickly, like millions of other couples in similar circumstances, they started a family, participating in the phenomenon aptly known as the "baby boom." The dream of a college education was put off for another generation.

My father's military service and the service of many other men from the Dutch immigrant community had one important, but sometimes overlooked feature. It meant that the Dutch immigrant community became almost entirely assimilated into American culture. My father and the other men of his generation thought of themselves as American citizens, and they were proud of it.

Not everyone who went to war came home, but those who did flew the U.S. flag proudly for the rest of their lives. The U.S. was their country in a way that it had not been before the war. They were the descendants of Dutch immigrants, yes, but their American identity had become the one that mattered most.

The language spoken by those first to arrive in Michigan had all but disappeared. I grew up in an American household, I heard only English spoken at home, and at school I pledged allegiance to the U.S. flag.

I was aware as I was growing up—an awareness that only grew over time and in fact became a weight of responsibility—that much of the dream of a Christian community in the U.S. was actually for me and my classmates. The Christian schools, the churches, and even the college I attended—this was the infrastructure that had been carefully and thoughtfully established for us. We were the beneficiaries of all that hard work.

My grandfather, Jay Brouwer, who quit school after the eighth grade, once told me that I should stay in school so that, as he put it, I wouldn't "have to work so hard." I thought that sounded odd at the time, because I was working as hard as I could, but later I came to understand what he meant.

He had worked hard at jobs I would never consider taking so that I could do more with my life than he had, so that I could go farther, and (as my mother liked to say) so that I could "make something" of myself.

That's what I think about all these years later: Have I made something of myself? Has my life amounted to anything? Have I been a grateful beneficiary of the work of Van Raalte and the others who came with him?

9

Sietze Buning and Calvinist Farming

"CALVINIST FARMING" MIGHT SEEM like an odd title for a poem, but then most of the poems by the Dutch American poet Sietze Buning have odd titles. A few of my favorites are: "Greasing the Windmill," "Barnyard Miracle," "Shivaree," and "The Valleys Stand So Thick With Corn."

What these poems have in common is their subject matter. Sietze Buning, the pseudonym of a Calvin College professor whose real name was Stanley Wiersma, wrote about the Dutch immigrant culture in which I was raised.

What he wrote about this culture would have been helpful and instructive, if only I had paid more attention earlier in my life, one of many regrets I have.

More than anything, Wiersma offered his readers a new way of seeing, which I suppose is what all good poets do. Where I was hyper-critical and unappreciative, he was fond and loving, always full of grace, even when it was clear that he saw the same stubbornness and rigidity in the immigrant culture that I did. One scholar has written that Wiersma's literary "voice" was one of "embarrassment and admiration, simplicity and sophistication."

Not everyone can embrace all of those things in one "voice."
Plenty of people grew up in the Dutch culture and left, and
after they left they never had much good to say about where they
came from. A few novelists and screenwriters who went to Calvin
College spent their entire careers, it seemed to me, writing conde-
scendingly about the college and the Dutch culture.

I remember a time when I took great pleasure in what they
wrote, especially writers like Frederick Manfred (whose real name
was Feike Feikema) and Peter DeVries. You might want to read
their books for yourselves. I still have just about everything they
ever wrote. If they ever saw anything good in the Dutch culture, it
was never more than grudging acknowledgment, and it was rare.

Wiersma, on the other hand, looked at the immigrant culture
in which he was raised and found humor, though he never poked
fun at it. If you read his poetry and laughed, you were really laugh-
ing at yourself. You were seeing yourself in the mirror he held in
front of you, which requires a kind of maturity I didn't have when
I first read his poetry.

"Calvinist Farming," for example, is a poem about plowing
fields, but not really.

The correct way to plow a field, according to nearly every
Dutch farmer in northwest Iowa, was to plow east to west in neat
rows. The rows could sometimes also run north to south for cross–
cultivation and weed control. Dutch farmers always plowed their
fields while wearing necktie, bib–overalls, and straw hat, a description that speaks volumes.

The way Dutch farmers planted their corn in the early years
of the twentieth century seemed right to them, and they were not
about to change. But a few of their neighbors began to adopt a
new American method, presumably suggested by the university
extension service. The new method was called "contour plowing,"
and I can imagine that those Dutch farmers kind of spit the words
as they spoke them, if they could bring themselves to speak them
at all. Instead of plowing straight over hills, which was the correct
way, the new way was to plow with the contour of the land.

Dutch farmers resisted the new way, thinking that if they went along with every new idea, they would be allowing themselves to be assimilated and absorbed into American culture. Contour plowing was for them a slippery slope.

Wiersma's readers knew that he was writing about more than plowing. He was writing about a way of life and how change came slowly, if at all, because change—any kind of change—might mean losing one's identity.

As I mentioned, I regret not paying more attention to that poem—and others like it—when I was younger.

At the time, all I could see in Dutch immigrant culture was how strange and backward it was. From what I have read, my feelings were typical of second- and third-generation immigrants. The headlong rush is always toward assimilation within the larger culture, leaving the immigrant culture behind as quickly as possible.

In my defense, I failed to see the logic of some of the rules I learned. The three vices of my childhood—the ones specifically condemned by the church—were dancing, card playing, and movie going. The prohibition against dancing was never much of a problem for me because I was never much of a dancer.

Card playing was one of the three that no one ever seemed to take seriously, at least not in my family. I was always envious of the way my father could shuffle a deck of cards, something he said he learned "in the service," and my grandmother, your great great–grandmother, Jessie Brouwer, often talked about playing a card game called canasta with her "girlfriends," which I thought was hilarious.

It was movie going that always seemed to be the most dangerous of the three. Movies, after all, were where I learned about the world beyond my own, which was bigger than I ever imagined, filled with beauty but also a great deal that was ugly. It was movie going that may have been the biggest factor in my urge to leave Grand Rapids and see the world for myself. It was certainly one factor leading me to move to Europe.

There were other rules and prohibitions too. Our family, for example, never watched television on Sunday because Sunday was the Sabbath.

An exception was made on a Sunday night in 1964 so we could watch the Beatles on "The Ed Sullivan Show." We hurried home from the evening service at church to see it. In hindsight, I don't think this rule was terribly oppressive. I always found other things to do, like reading books, but as with most of the rules and prohibitions, there was never much of an explanation. It was never clear how following these rules made us better people. I saw only how they made us different.

Like resistance to contour plowing, I now think that the abundance of rules and prohibitions was mostly about preserving our immigrant culture and its identity, which everyone could see was slipping away.

My biggest and most painful conflict with this culture occurred in connection with the Vietnam War.

To be fair, the 1960s and 1970s were challenging to the Dutch in the U.S., as they were challenging for just about everybody. The war, the civil rights movement, campus unrest, urban riots, Watergate, the assassinations of public figures like John F. Kennedy, Robert F. Kennedy, and Martin Luther King, Jr.—these were all in various ways a challenge to the identity of the culture in which I was raised.

But it was the Vietnam War that affected me most deeply. I was seventeen years old when I realized that I would soon be drafted into the army and sent to Vietnam. My draft lottery number was nine, meaning I would be among the first called up as soon as I turned eighteen. Nothing in my life before or after has ever focused my attention the way this did.

I couldn't think of anything in the sermons I had heard while I was growing up or in the Sunday school classes I had attended that would support war. In fact, just the opposite was true. What I had been taught was that war was wrong. War was evidence of a sinful and fallen world, one in need of redemption.

You could argue that my thinking about this was my own version of Calvinist farming—my own version of the stubbornness and rigidity I saw all around me. I became convinced that this issue was where I needed to take a stand. I read widely, I thought hard, and I even got on my knees and prayed. I decided to become a conscientious objector.

This decision was upsetting to my parents, as you can perhaps imagine, since my father had volunteered to serve during World War II.

Conscientious objection to military service was allowed at the time, but only on religious grounds, and neither my pastor nor my church was enthusiastic about my decision. My church was reluctant to take a stand on the Vietnam War. It was inclined instead to support the U.S. government and its foreign policy. My pastor told me he would not attend the meeting of the draft board where I would have to make my case. My prospects therefore looked bleak.

But like the Calvinist farmers in Wiersma's poetry I was stubborn. I made the best case I could to the draft board, and in the end, to my surprise, I was granted the conscientious objector classification.

In that series of events, I believed the immigrant culture in which I was raised had let me down and abandoned its own beliefs. For many years I could not think fondly and appreciatively of it.

Sietze Buning is the pseudonym of Dr. Stanley Wiersma (1925-2011).

CALVINIST FARMING

Our Calvinist fathers wore neckties with their bib–overalls
and straw hats, a touch of glory with their humility. They rode
their horse–drawn corn planters like chariots, planting the corn
in straight rows, each hill of three stalks three from each hill
around it, up and over the rises. A field–length wire with a metal knot
every three feet ran through the planter and clicked off three kernels
at each knot. Planted in rows east-west, the rows also ran north-
south for cross–cultivating. Each field was a checkerboard even
to the diagonals. No Calvinist followed the land's contours.

Contour farmers in surrounding counties
improvised their rows against the slope
of the land. There was no right way.
Before our fathers planted a field,
they knew where each hill of corn
would be. Be ye perfect, God said,
and the trouble with contour farmers
was that, no matter how hard they worked
at getting a perfect contour, they could
never know for sure it was perfect—and
they didn't even care. At best they
were Arminian, or Lutheran, or Catholic,
or at worst secular. Though they wore bib-
overalls, they wore no neckties, humility
without glory.
                              Contour fields resulted
from free will, nary a cornstalk predetermined. The God contour farmers
trusted, if any, was as capricious
as their cornfields. Calvinists knew
the distance between God and people was
even greater than the distance between people
and corn kernels. If we were corn kernels in God's
corn planter, would we want him to plan us at random?

Contour farmers were frivolous about the doctrine of election
simply by being contour famers.

Contour farmers didn't control
weeds because they couldn't cross-cultivate. Weed control was laid
on farmers by God's curse. Contour farmers tried to escape God's curse.
Sooner or later you could tell it on their children: condoning weeds
they condoned movies and square-skipping. And they wasted land,
for planting around the rises, they left more place between
the rows than if they'd checked it. It was all indecent.
We could drive a horse cultivator—it was harder
with a tractor cultivator—through our checked rows
without uprooting any corn at all, but contour farmers
could never quite recapture the arbitrary angle, cultivating,
that they used, planting. They uprooted corn and killed it. All
of it was indecent and untidy.

We youngsters pointed out that the tops
of our rises were turning clay–brown, that bushels of black dirt
washed into creeks and ditches every time it rained, and that
in the non–Calvinist counties the tops of the rises were
black. We were told we were arguing by results, not
by principles. Why, God could replenish the black
dirt overnight. The tops of the rises were God's business.
Our business was to farm on Biblical principles.
Like, Let everything be done decently and in good order; that is
keep weeds down, plant every square inch, do not waste crops, and be
tidy.
Contour farmers were unkingly because they were untidy. They could not
be
Prophetic, could not explain from the Bible how to farm. Being neither
kings
nor prophets, they could not be proper priests; their humility lacked defi-
nition. They prayed for crops privately. Our while county prayed
for crops the second Wednesday of every March.

God's cosmic planter
has planted thirty years's worth of people since then,
all checked out and on the diagonal if we could see

as God sees. All third-generation Calvinists
now plant corn on the contour. They have the word
from the State College of Agriculture. And so the clay-
brown has stopped spreading farther down the rises
and life has not turned secular, but broken.

                                                                  For

God still plants people on the predetermined check
even though Calvinists plant corn on the contour. God's
check doesn't mean a kernel in the Calvinist's cornfield.
There's no easy way to tell the difference between Calvinists
and non-Calvinists: now all plant on the contour; all tolerate
weeds; between rows, all waste space; all uproot corn, cultivating;
all consider erosion their own business, not God's; all wear
overalls without ties; all their children go to the same
movies and dances; the county's prayer meetings
in March are badly attended; and I am improvising
this poem on the contour, not checking it in rhyme.
Glad for the new freedom, I miss the old freedom of choice
between Calvinist and non-Calvinist farming. Only in religion
are Calvinist and non-Calvinist distinguishable now. When different
ideas of God produced different methods of farming. God mattered more.
Was the old freedom worth giving up for the new? Did stopping the old
erosion of earth start a new erosion of spirit? Was stopping old
erosion worth the pain of new brokenness? The old Calvinists
insisted that the only hope for unbrokenness between the ways
of God and the ways of farmers is God.

                                      A priest, God wears
infinite humility; a king, he wears infinite glory. He is even
less influenced by his upward-mobile children's notions of what not
to wear with what than our Calvinist fathers were in neckties with bib-
overalls. Moreover, a prophet, he wears the infinite truth our Calvinist
father's hankered after to vindicate themselves, not only their farming.
Just wait, some dark night God will ride over the rises on his chariot-
corn planter. It will be too dark to tell his crown from a straw hat,
too dark to tell his apocalyptic horses from our buckskin horses or
from unicorns. No matter, just so the wheels of that chariot-corn

planter, dropping fatness, churn up all those clay–brown rises
and turn them all black, just as the old Calvinists predicted.

Lord Jesus, come quickly.

10

What Is Your Only Comfort?

WHEN I WAS IN third grade I started to attend weekly catechism classes at my church, something I would do until I graduated from high school. At the time I thought children all over the world did pretty much the same thing.

In catechism classes we memorized the 129 questions and answers of the Heidelberg Catechism, a doctrinal statement published in 1653, in a city called Heidelberg, in what is now Germany. It's a lovely medieval city. I have been there, and I hope you are able to visit someday as well.

Why an eight—or nine—year-old child would be expected to memorize words written roughly 400 years before he was born is what this part of my letter to you is about. You might be surprised to know that, looking back, I am grateful for the experience.

As I mentioned in a previous chapter, I am descended from Dutch people who immigrated for both economic and religious reasons. They were hoping for a better life, but to them "better" meant more than having an income and employment and enough to eat. To them "better" meant having the opportunity to fully embrace their strict interpretation of the Calvinist faith.

You would have to grow up among these people, as I did, to appreciate how fiercely they fought for what they believed, including seemingly insignificant bits of doctrine. People like my grandparents and great-grandparents, who had no formal education beyond the eighth grade, knew how to hold their own in a theological debate. They didn't hesitate to correct a pastor, either, thinking that the pastor's theological training was itself a reason to be suspicious.

I clearly remember a time when my "Grandpa Pete," who was my grandmother Minnie's second husband, left a church service one Sunday night in the middle of the sermon. He stormed noisily out of the church by way of the center aisle, muttering "Storyteller!" under his breath, but still loudly enough so everyone could hear him. Even as I child I knew that this word was uttered in anger and directed toward the preacher.

I also remember hearing my grandmother whisper in response, somewhat embarrassed, and probably exasperated, "Oh, Pete!"

She did not follow him out of the church.

The issue, I learned later in the evening, after asking a few questions, was that my grandfather wanted doctrine in the sermons he heard, not sentimentality. He wanted the truth presented in a straightforward, no-nonsense manner, just as it was presented in the Heidelberg Catechism, which he surely knew as well as anyone in the church, including the preacher. And any preacher who added superfluous words—or homely anecdotes—wasn't worth his time.

That was just my mother's side of the family.

On my father's side there was as much debate, though it was somewhat less volatile, perhaps out of necessity, with a young child around. When my father's grandfather, Henry Vander Veen, became a widower, he went to live with his daughter Jessie and her husband, Jay Brouwer. Henry was a member of the Protestant Reformed Church, Jessie was a member of the Christian Reformed Church, and Jay was a member of the Reformed Church in America, making for a toxic brew of different church allegiances in one household.

My father, like all children in situations of family conflict, was mostly a silent observer of what was happening around him. I like to think he first started to paint idyllic rural landscapes during this period of his life. He seemed to find great comfort in his painting throughout his life.

To explain the situation, maybe it's easiest to begin with my grandfather Jay. His denomination, the RCA, was the first to abandon the singing of Psalms in the Dutch language. The RCA was also, as I recall, somewhat lax in its attitude toward Masonic lodge membership. There must have been other perceived deficiencies about the RCA as well. What all of this meant, of course, was that my grandfather Jay was willing to accommodate and assimilate and therefore let go of much that made the new immigrants distinctive within American culture.

My great-grandfather Henry's denomination, the PRC, broke away from the CRC on the matter of common grace, which is far too complicated to explain here. Whatever the particulars, it must have been quite a fight, and for my family, as well as the Dutch immigrant community, the stakes would have been high, even though the actual theological differences between all of them now seem relatively small.

In 1924, a year before my father was born, the PRC broke away from the CRC to found its own sectarian brand of the Reformed faith, and my great-grandfather, Henry, proudly went along. If the family was wounded or thrown into conflict by taking this stand, then to him that was a price he was willing to pay.

I'm not sure what role my grandmother, Jessie, played within the household. She seems to have taken up the moderate position—if the CRC can be considered moderate, which not many people think it is—but she was a strong person and would not have kept quiet about her opinions. It's possible that women did not, as a rule, express themselves on these or other matters, except in the privacy of their own homes.

Only later in my life, after I had moved far from Grand Rapids, did I learn that most Christian people, those from other theological traditions, did not grow up in doctrine-obsessed households.

Frankly, I felt superior to these other Christians, at least at first, because I had learned the language of doctrinal debate so much earlier in my life. Memorizing the Heidelberg Catechism, I have to say, gave me the feeling that I knew more than I did.

It's ironic, when you think about it, because the Heidelberg Catechism is mostly a peaceful document. A few unfortunate sentences in the catechism notwithstanding, it has a good spirit overall and has rightly been called a "catechism of comfort." The German prince who oversaw the writing of it and who likely wrote its introduction was himself a Lutheran—with some strong Reformed leanings—but the overall intent seemed to be to find common ground.

Today, several different denominations in the U.S. and around the world embrace the catechism as authoritative for their beliefs, even if they don't always like each other very much.

By the time I was in high school I finally had the thing memorized. Standing in front of the church elders, with my classmates, many of whom had been with me since the third grade, I could recite the answers to the questions we were asked as well as any of them.

Today, I don't remember the catechism quite as well—a few key phrases, maybe, but not the whole thing, certainly not word for word. And yet, the catechism, to which I gave hours and hours of my time, both at church and at home (where my parents reinforced my memory work) is imprinted on my life. In large ways, and small, it tells me who I am.

The first question and answer of the catechism (which I can still say from memory) lies at the heart of my faith. I never fail to get tears in my eyes when I say the words. This is the faith that my parents and grandparents and great-grandparents passed on to me, and I am grateful to them:

Q. What is your only comfort in life and in death?
A. That I am not my own, but belong—body and soul, in life and in death—to my faithful Savior, Jesus Christ. He has fully paid for all my sins with his precious blood, and has set me free from

the tyranny of the devil. He also watches over me in such a way that not a hair can fall from my head without the will of my Father in heaven; in fact, all things must work together for my salvation. Because I belong to him, Christ, by his Holy Spirit, assures me of eternal life and makes me wholeheartedly willing and ready from now on to live for him.

Henry Vander Veen and his first wife, who later died in child birth, with a few of their children—Alice, Andrew, and Jessie, who was to become my grandmother.

11

James A. Brouwer and the Electric Car

To this point I've written mostly about ancestors who came to the United States and, against long odds, not only survived but thrived, making me proud to be descended from them. That was meant to be an inspiring story for you, as it has been for me.

But the story is more complicated than that, as you must have recognized by this point. The separatist spirit that brought Dutch immigrants to the United States was sincere enough, but it could also be stubborn, rigid, and intolerant.

I have found no stories from those who remained in the Netherlands about how they were sad to see the separatists leave. Divorce, which this surely was, is painful in any circumstances, but I can imagine that the state church breathed a sigh of relief with every departing ship.

What was unexpected to me about this history is that, given the immigrants' desire to preserve their culture and beliefs, they were at the same time in a rush to be assimilated within American culture. The name changes I mentioned in a previous chapter, such as my grandmother's name change from Jacomina to Minnie, were certainly heroic at one level but utterly practical at another. As much as the Dutch immigrants were suspicious of American culture, as much as they kept their distance from it, as much as they railed against its many shortcomings, they nevertheless longed to be accepted by it.

To dig deeper, I want to tell the story of Jacobus Apolonius Brouwer, who is better known in western Michigan as James A. Brouwer.

You probably didn't know that your grandmother is also descended from a person named Brouwer, but don't be alarmed: Your grandmother and I are not second cousins. As I explained in a previous chapter, lots of Dutch villages in the 19th century had Brouwers, just as they had Bakkers, Vissers, de Jongs, de Boers, and so on. In spite of having the same last name, few of these people were related.

Still, I think it's interesting that there are Brouwers on your grandmother's side of the family, and I think you should know about them—one in particular, and the important role he played in Holland's business, civic, and church life, all the way into the mid–twentieth century.

James Brouwer was born on February 20, 1854, at 6 p.m. I'm not sure why the time of his birth is important, but that's how he tells the story in a document he wrote called "History of Our Family Record—as much as I could obtain or recall in February 1936." It's a fascinating document—part autobiography, part family tree, not so different from what I've written here, though much shorter.

In any case, a great deal is known about James Brouwer and his life, including the exact time of his birth, because at age eighty he decided to tell his story. Most of what he writes sounds reliable, but you should know that I have been unable to corroborate all of the names and dates (and precise times of birth) he provides.

James Brouwer reports that his father, Willem, was born in Arnhem in 1812. His mother, Gertrude Johanna de Waal, was born in Delft in 1817. They were married in Arnhem, which is in the Dutch province known as Gelderland.

Like the members of my own family who immigrated to the United States, your grandmother's ancestors were also separatists who rejected the state church in the Netherlands. But as James Brouwer tells the story, the decision to "join the secession had economic consequences," which is something of an understatement in the case of his parents. Willem Brouwer—a tailor, not a brewer—had a small shop and seven employees, and with his decision he lost all of his customers and, shortly thereafter, his business.

"Rather than denying their faith," as James Brouwer tells the story, Willem and Gertrude set out for America, "where they could serve God according to the dictates of their own consciences."

I am inclined to trust this description because it is similar to so many other stories from the same period. The state church in the Netherlands, the Hervormde Kerk, "originally sound in doctrine," became "so modernistic" that many of its members, including my ancestors and those of your grandmother, made the decision to join the wave of immigrants who were leaving Europe at the time.

The cost to the separatists was not only economic but personal. Gertrude's brother, Jacobus Gerardus de Waal, a physician, "was so displeased" with his sister's decision to go to America that "he refused to reply to the many letters she wrote him from America."

James Brouwer, Gertrude's son, adds this comment about his uncle, which he must have heard more than once from his mother: "[Jacobus] seemed adverse to religion." It's a cutting comment, but it reflects the zeal of those who left. If blame for the broken relationship were to be assigned, it would be assigned to the brother who apparently didn't take his faith seriously enough.

My inclination through much of my genealogical research has been to admire my ancestors, and there is no denying their courage and the sacrifices they made. More than once, knowing how difficult it is to set out on a journey, I have wondered if I would have been able to do what they did. But the separatist spirit did not disappear after the arrival in the United States. Breaks, schisms, and separations—ecclesiastical and personal—continued to occur.

Doctrinal error was a serious matter. Being right was nearly always more important than getting along.

Willem and Gertrude, according to their son's account, arrived first in New Orleans, where Willem briefly and unsuccessfully tried to duplicate his previous success in the tailoring business. Within a year, he and Gertrude, having heard about the Dutch colony founded by Albertus Van Raalte in Michigan, decided to set out again. In 1848, only a year after Van Raalte established the Holland settlement, Willem and Gertrude arrived with a hundred dollars and "lived in with others where they could find shelter."

In what is now downtown Holland—at the intersection of 8th Street and College Avenue—Willem and Gertrude bought a lot from Van Raalte for forty-eight dollars. There they planted apple trees, dug a well, built a small home, and started a family, producing seven children in rapid succession. Sadly, four of the seven did not live beyond childhood.

Jacobus Apolonius—who later changed his name to James for reasons he does not provide—was born in 1854, lived to be nearly ninety–seven, and became one of the most colorful characters in Holland's early history. His great–grandchildren describe him, when he was in his nineties, as a "kindly old man with twinkling eyes."

In 1864, when James Brouwer was ten years old, his mother "concluded that it was her duty to sever her relationship with the Reformed Church since some of their ministers taught unreformed doctrine," though the exact nature of this doctrinal deviation is not mentioned. The nearest Christian Reformed Church–"then called the True Reformed Church," according to James Brouwer's account—was in Graafschap, a walk of four miles from their home in Holland, perhaps a pleasant walk on sunny days but undoubtedly a slog in winter months.

James' father, interestingly, consented to Gertrude's decision "to sever her relationship," but he decided to remain in the Reformed Church. Again, no additional information is provided about what must have been quite a serious discussion between husband and wife.

At age eleven James Brouwer went to work full-time, and by age fifteeen he was apprenticed to a furniture and cabinet maker, starting at three dollars per week and gradually rising to six dollars for a sixty-hour week.

"This was hard work," he admits, but he quickly learned all phases of the business, including sales and marketing, eventually establishing the Jas. A. Brouwer Furniture Co., which was something of a landmark in downtown Holland. The "showroom" would eventually include one of the first elevators in the city, so shoppers would not have to trudge all the way up to the third floor.

James Brouwer married Gezina Noordhuis "of Grand Haven" in 1881. Less than a year later, they "were gladdened by the birth of a daughter," named Gertrude Johanna after her grandmother. She lived only three years and four months, however, and James Brouwer writes that "this was a loss no one can understand that has not experienced it," which is a succinct and touching description of the death of a child, one I have heard several times in my work over the years. "We were very much cast down and gloomy. We could not stand to see anyone joyful or singing."

This first child was followed by three more girls, including a set of twins, and finally two boys.

In his account James Brouwer modestly states that "our business kept growing," as though this came as a surprise or without much effort on his part, but the truth is that he in time became one of the most prominent business owners in Holland, active also in civic and church affairs, serving in leadership roles. His electric car, the first of its kind in Holland, a 1925 Detroit Electric, added to his legend as a colorful figure, and newspaper photos suggest he was also exceptionally well-dressed, further evidence of his financial success.

The account of his life concludes with these words: "The Lord has greatly favored me, an unworthy sinful man. I cannot account for His goodness ... but humbly bow before Him believing that He is an all–wise God." I suppose I could say the same about my own life.

Though I am not related to this man, except through your grandmother, I find that I have inherited a great deal from him, an odd and perplexing blend of characteristics: humility and yet a stubborn belief that I am right about most doctrinal matters; courage and then tenderness and frequently tears in the face of death; deep piety with more than a little earthiness; and finally an inner determination to work harder and longer than anyone else in order to succeed.

These qualities, found in James Brouwer and in many of the second- and third-generation immigrants, have shaped who I am far more than any genetic material.

History of our Family Record as much as I could obtain
or recall in February 1936.

Father's name was Willem Brouwer. Born in Arnhem, Netherlands, Europe, July 18th, 1812. He had a brother named Frederick who was some older than he. Father corresponded with him once in a while, so when Father died we wrote him about it but we never received a reply. It is possible that he also died by that time. I never heard Father speak about his parents or family, therefore know nothing about them.

Mother's name was Gertrude Johanna De Waal. She was born in Delft, Netherlands, Europe Jan. 8th, 1817 at 8:00 P. M.

Her Grandfather De Waal was a school teacher.

Her Grandmother died when Mother was six years old. Mother remembered well how she spoke a word to everyone present at her deathbed, and when Mother's turn came, she said, "Gertrude, pray at all times". Then she smiled, raised her eyes, stretched out her arms, and said, "There is my Jesus" and fell asleep.

Mother's Grandparents on her Mother's side died before she was born.

Mother's Father's name was Jacobus De Waal. He gave private lessons at the homes of well-to-do people, but being troubled with asthma when he grew older he had to discontinue, and was appointed commissioner of the Delft Harbor Transportation to Rotterdam. This office he retained until he died. He died of cancer in his tongue at the age of 70.

Mother was then seventeen years old. She had been with her Father continually. Her Mother died when she was nine years. After her Father died till she married she stayed with people in comfortable circumstances as ladies' companion.

Mother's Father had two sisters, one a linen seamstress, the other a woolen seamstress, and two brothers, one a carpenter, and the other a sailor.

The name of Mother's Mother was Gertruida Schouman, and was born in Dortrecht, whose father was a "Beurt Shipper" (meaning a conveyor by water of inland package freight) between Dortrecht and den Briel. He died when 52 years old.

Her mother had two brothers, one was a house painter, and the other an artist, painting landscapes and water scenery on canvass and panel; and his son also an artist painting portraits from life on canvass or panel. A large portrait painted by him of Mother's Father can be seen in the home of cousin J. A. G. De Waal in Kampen, Netherlands. His daughter was a painter on china.

A cousin of Mother's Father was a teacher in French in connection with his French Boarding School, another cousin was an officer in the war with Belguim in 1830. His home was in Delft.

Mother had two brothers. The older, Jacobus Gerardus De Waal was medical doctor in Middelburg, and had a son named Johannes. We know very little about him. He was so displeased with Mother going to America that he refused to reply to the many letters she wrote him from America. He also seemed adverse to religion.

"History of Our Family Record" by James A. Brouwer (first page).

12

I Was Born a Baby

I HAVE A DEAR friend who taught me something important about my identity, and I will never forget it.

But first I should tell you something about *his* identity, which makes what he taught me all the more memorable. You should know first that he was born in what is now Israel. When he was born, in 1939, the land was called Palestine.

He's an Arab, which I learned is more about language than race or ethnicity, though these things, as you can imagine, can get quite complicated. He speaks Arabic, as did his parents and his brothers and sisters, but he now speaks several other languages as well. When he was growing up, he spoke Arabic at home and church, he learned Hebrew and English in school, and then later at university in Paris he learned French and maybe one or two others.

His name is Elias Chacour, and he is a Melkite priest and an Arab Christian. He retired not long ago after eight years as archbishop of Galilee. I first came to know him not as an archbishop, but as the founder of a school in Galilee for Christian, Muslim, and Jewish children. I have visited his school several times and have been on the rooftop of his home late into the evening for conversation. He has made quite an impression on me and how I think of my life and work. Inspired by his example, I have tried to demonstrate more courage and strength in my work, even though I know that our situations are vastly different.

During one of our conversations, he said that he is often asked how he became a Christian. People want to know if he was "born a Christian," because apparently they are surprised to meet an Arab in the Middle East who is not a Muslim. So in response he always says something funny and disarming but also truthful and worth remembering.

He says, "I was born a baby."

In other words, he wants people to know that we have this one thing in common. All of us were born babies; we are human beings, first of all, created in the image and likeness of God. We didn't start out as Christians, Muslims, or Jews. Or Dutch, or Chinese, or Indian, for that matter. We all started out as babies. It is our most basic identity, and it is one that's easy to forget.

I mentioned in the chapter about DNA that our genetic material cannot tell us our race or ethnicity. But that's not quite true. DNA can tell us a great deal about our ancestors and exactly what social group they identified with. In that sense, DNA is often a terrific predictor of race and ethnicity.

But my DNA is not what makes me Dutch. I now know, without much doubt, that I descended from people who lived for centuries in northern Europe, in a region that is now the Netherlands, but I don't live there. I never have. Neither did my mother and father. I was born several thousand miles away from there—on the continent of North America. Beyond that, I speak no more than a few Dutch words, and I probably mispronounce most of those.

Still, I have regularly told people over the years that I am Dutch. People I meet who actually are from the Netherlands are usually quite amused to hear me say that, and often they wonder aloud what that might mean. I have to admit it's a difficult question to answer. I think of myself as Dutch mostly because I want it to be true.

Human beings seem to have a powerful need to know where they came from, and then that information shapes their identity in some profound ways.

Back in 1976, before your parents were born, an African-American man named Alex Haley wrote a 900-page book called *Roots*, which became a best-seller. A weeklong TV series, based on the book, was broadcast the following year, and a record-breaking number of people watched it.

What Haley had done was what no one thought possible at the time. He traced the ancestry of his family to 18th century Gambia. You can't imagine how thrilling it was—at last—that there was a history that reached back to the days before slavery. Slaves were counted but almost never named in the U.S. census prior to 1870, so that's regrettably where most family histories stopped.

The publication of *Roots* and the broadcast of the mini-series were the spark for many, many other people to search for their own roots and their own unique histories. Henry Louis Gates, Jr., is a Harvard professor and historian, and it was Haley's book that set Gates on his own search for ancestors.

At the time he knew nothing about his family history before his great-great-grandmother, a former slave who had lived from 1819 to 1888, but Gates found he could trace his ancestry to Sudan. He discovered that he is Nubian and that his family members were rulers in Egypt many centuries ago. He was surprised and delighted with the information. His identity, his sense of himself, grew.

Interestingly, DNA testing later determined that Gates is also Irish. His great-great-grandmother's children were fathered by a man of Irish descent, even though Gates has always identified as African American. With that discovery, as you can imagine, his identity grew once again, in an unexpected direction.

Most people, I would say, wonder about who they are and where they came from. Some are more obsessive about finding answers than others, but all of us wonder about our stories and our family histories. The information we gather, the family legends we research, all of it comes together to form an identity, a sense of self.

We all construct a picture for ourselves of who we are. I've done it, your parents will do it, and I suspect that soon, if you haven't already started, you will begin to do it. You will find a way to describe yourself that will draw from what you have learned about yourself and your past.

But here's what I want you to see: Family histories and genealogies and DNA testing can be fun and interesting and occasionally enlightening, but in the end they can't tell us everything we need to know about ourselves.

For several months I worked feverishly at my laptop, sometimes late into the night, to construct my family tree. I spit into a glass tube, as I mentioned, and had my DNA tested. I interviewed my mother and several other people, who might have some knowledge about my family history. I even wandered around an old cemetery for most of an afternoon, searching for grave markers with my family name.

What prompted all of the searching and digging and study was a desire to answer one of the most basic questions there is: Who am I?

Of course I already knew who I was. You don't get to be 60 years old and not have a pretty good idea. Still, I was busy for most of those years. I went to school for a lot of years, probably more than was necessary. I worked hard at a job that I loved, but that demanded a lot of my time. I also tried my best through all of that to be a good husband and a good father.

So when I reached the age when I could retire, I found myself wanting to know once again who I am, who I really am, the truth about me.

I am a pastor, yes, and even though I wasn't always sure what that meant, especially at the beginning, I gradually grew into the role. In fact, it was more than a role. It turned out to be a way of life. Ask your parents. It was a way of life that drew our entire family into it. We couldn't escape if we wanted to, and mostly I think we didn't want to. It was a good and rich life. Even so, I am more than a pastor.

I am also a husband and father, two roles I loved more than anything I have done with my life—rather unexpectedly, I have to say, because I didn't grow up imagining myself as one or the other.

When your parents left for college, I thought I would never recover from the sadness of it, even though they were doing exactly what I had always wanted for them. I had embraced the identity of a father so fully that I couldn't bear to let them go.

And now I am a grandfather, another unexpected thrill, better than I could ever have imagined. But being a husband and father and grandfather still isn't the whole story—the truth—about me.

As my research and study comes to an end, I now see that the answer to my question is a rather simple one.

I was born a baby.

That is the truth about me. That is my identity, and it is the only one that matters, the one on which all the others rest. Because I understood myself to be a child of God, I became a pastor. Because I was created in the image and likeness of God, I could also be a husband and father and grandfather. Because I was born a baby, I could be a human being and a friend to all.

Please remember that. You were born a baby. You are a child of God. I think it's pretty much all you need to know about yourself.

Made in the USA
Middletown, DE
08 November 2020